BARACK OBAMA biography
bio book

by David Right

PREFACE

Barack Obama has a special place in history as he is the first African American president of USA. Born in Honolulu to Ann Durham and Barack Obama Sr., Obama served as Illinois Senator for a time period of approximately three and a half year from January 2005 - November 2008. As soon as he was elected as the President of the United States, he resigned from his post of Senator.

He has an advantage of experience in foreign countries, a patch-work of cultures and places in his background. He can blend in anywhere, identify with anybody, and connect with both sides across almost any chasm.

Table of Contents

CHAPTER 1- THE BIOGRAPHY OF BARACK OBAMA

Barack Obama was the 44th president of the United States, and the first African American to serve in the office. First elected to the presidency in 2008, he won a second term in 2012.

"I am not opposed to all wars. I'm opposed to dumb wars."

—Barack Obama

Synopsis

Born in Honolulu in 1961, Barack Obama went on to become President of the Harvard Law Review and a U.S. senator representing Illinois. In 2008, he was elected President of the United States, becoming the first African-American commander-in-chief. He served two terms as the 44 president of the United States.

Early Life

Barack Hussein Obama II was born on August 4, 1961, in Honolulu, Hawaii. His mother, Ann Dunham, was born on an Army base in Wichita, Kansas, during World War II. After the Japanese attack on Pearl Harbor, Dunham's father, Stanley, enlisted in the military and marched across Europe in General George Patton's army. Dunham's mother, Madelyn, went to work on a bomber assembly line. After the war, the couple studied on the G.I. Bill, bought a house through the Federal Housing Program and, after several moves, ended up in Hawaii.

Obama's father, Barack Obama Sr., was born of Luo ethnicity in Nyanza Province, Kenya. Obama Sr. grew up herding goats in Africa and, eventually earned a scholarship that allowed him to leave Kenya and pursue his dreams of going to college in Hawaii. While studying at the University of Hawaii at Manoa,

Obama Sr. met fellow student Ann Dunham, and they married on February 2, 1961. Barack was born six months later.

As a child, Obama did not have a relationship with his father. When his son was still an infant, Obama Sr. relocated to Massachusetts to attend Harvard University and pursue a Ph.D. Obama's parents officially separated several months later and ultimately divorced in March 1964, when their son was two. Soon after, Obama Sr. returned to Kenya.

In 1965, Dunham married Lolo Soetoro, a University of Hawaii student from Indonesia. A year later, the family moved to Jakarta, Indonesia, where Obama's half-sister, Maya Soetoro Ng, was born in 1970. Several incidents in Indonesia left Dunham afraid for her son's safety and education so, at the age of 10, Obama was sent back to Hawaii to live with his maternal grandparents. His mother and half-sister later joined them.

Education

While living with his grandparents, Obama enrolled in the esteemed Punahou Academy, He excelled in basketball and graduated with academic honors in 1979. As one of only three black students at the school, Obama became conscious of racism and what it meant to be African-American. He later described how he struggled to reconcile social perceptions of his multiracial heritage with his own sense of self: "I noticed that there was nobody like me in the Sears, Roebuck Christmas catalog and that Santa was a white man," he wrote. "I went into the bathroom and stood in front of the mirror with all my senses and limbs seemingly intact, looking as I had always looked, and wondered if something was wrong with me."

Obama also struggled with the absence of his father, who he saw only once more after his parents divorced, when Obama Sr. visited Hawaii for a short time in 1971. "My father had left paradise, and nothing that my mother or grandparents told me could obviate that single, unassailable fact," he later reflected. "They could not describe what it might have been like had he stayed."

Ten years later, in 1981, tragedy struck Obama Sr. when he lost both of his legs in a serious car accident. Confined to a wheelchair, he also lost his job. In 1982, Obama Sr. was involved in yet another car accident while traveling in Nairobi. This time, however, the crash was fatal. Obama Sr. died on November 24, 1982, when Obama was 21 years old. "At the time of his death, my father remained a myth to me," Obama later wrote, "both more and less than a man."

After high school, Obama studied at Occidental College in Los Angeles for two years. He then transferred to Columbia University in New York City, graduating in 1983 with a degree in political science. After working in the business sector for two years, Obama moved to Chicago in 1985. There, he worked on the impoverished South Side as a community organizer for low-income residents in the Roseland and the Altgeld Gardens communities.

Law Career

It was during this time that Obama, who said he "was not raised in a religious household," joined the Trinity United Church of Christ. He also visited relatives in Kenya and paid an emotional visit to the graves of his biological father and paternal grandfather. "For a long time, I sat between the two graves and wept," Obama wrote. "I saw that my life in America—the black life, the white life, the sense of abandonment I'd felt as a boy, the frustration and hope I'd witnessed in Chicago—all of it was connected with this small plot of earth an ocean away."

Returning from Kenya with a sense of renewal, Obama entered Harvard Law School in 1988. The next year, he met with constitutional law professor Laurence Tribe and their discussion so impressed Tribe, that when Obama asked to join his team as a research assistant, the professor agreed. "The better he did at Harvard Law School and the more he impressed people, the more obvious it

8

became that he could have had anything, said Professor Tribe in a 2012 interview with Frontline, "but it was clear that he wanted to make a difference to people, to communities." That same year Obama joined the Chicago law firm of Sidley Austin as a summer associate and it was there he met Michelle Robinson, a young lawyer who was assigned to be his adviser. Not long after, the couple began dating. In February 1990, Obama was elected the first African-American editor of the Harvard Law Review. He graduated magna cum laude from Harvard Law in 1991.

After law school, Obama returned to Chicago to practice as a civil rights lawyer with the firm of Miner, Barnhill & Galland. He also taught constitutional law part-time at the University of Chicago Law School between 1992 and 2004—first as a lecturer and then as a professor—and helped organize voter registration drives during Bill Clinton's 1992 presidential campaign. On October 3, 1992, he and Michelle were married. They moved to Kenwood, on Chicago's South Side, and welcomed two daughters several years later: Malia (born 1998) and Sasha (born 2001).

Entry Into Illinois Politics

Obama published an autobiography, Dreams from My Father: A Story of Race and Inheritance, in 1995. The work received high praise from literary figures such as Toni Morrison and has since been printed in more than 25 languages, including Chinese, Swedish and Hebrew. The book had a second printing in 2004 and was adapted for a children's version. The audiobook version of Dreams, narrated by Obama, received a Grammy Award for best spoken word album in 2006.

Obama's advocacy work led him to run for a seat in the Illinois State Senate. He ran as a Democrat and won the election in 1996. During his years as a state senator, Obama worked with both Democrats and Republicans to draft legislation on ethics, as well as expand health care services and early childhood education programs for the poor. He also created a state earned-income tax credit for the working poor. As chairman of the Illinois Senate's Health and Human Services Committee Obama worked with law enforcement officials to re□uire the videotaping of interrogations and confessions in all capital cases after a number of death-row inmates were found to be innocent.

In 2000, Obama made an unsuccessful Democratic primary run for the U.S. House of Representatives seat held by four-term incumbent candidate Bobby Rush. Undeterred, he created a campaign committee in 2002 and began raising funds to run for a seat in the U.S. Senate in 2004. With the help of political consultant David Axelrod, Obama began assessing his prospects for a Senate win.

Following the 9/11 attacks in 2001, Obama was an early opponent of President George W. Bush's push to go to war with Ira□. Obama was still a state senator when he spoke against a resolution authorizing the use of force against Ira□ during a rally at Chicago's Federal Plaza in October 2002. "I am not opposed to all wars. I'm opposed to dumb wars," he said. "What I am opposed to is the cynical attempt by Richard Perle and Paul Wolfowitz and other armchair, weekend warriors in this administration to shove their own ideological agendas down our throats, irrespective of the costs in lives lost and in hardships borne." Despite his protests, the Ira□ War began in 2003.

U.S. Senate Career

Encouraged by poll numbers, Obama decided to run for the U.S. Senate open seat vacated by Republican Peter Fitzgerald. In the 2004 Democratic primary, he defeated multimillionaire businessman Blair Hull and Illinois Comptroller Daniel Hynes with 52 percent of the vote. That summer, he was invited to deliver the keynote speech in support of John Kerry at the 2004 Democratic National Convention in Boston. Obama emphasized the importance

10

of unity and made veiled jabs at the Bush administration and the diversionary use of wedge issues.

After the convention, Obama returned to his U.S. Senate bid in Illinois. His opponent in the general election was supposed to be Republican primary winner Jack Ryan, a wealthy former investment banker. However, Ryan withdrew from the race in June 2004 following public disclosure of unsubstantiated sexual deviancy allegations by his ex-wife, actress Jeri Ryan.

In August 2004, diplomat and former presidential candidate Alan Keyes accepted the Republican nomination to replace Ryan. In three televised debates, Obama and Keyes expressed opposing views on stem cell research, abortion, gun control, school vouchers and tax cuts. In the November 2004 general election, Obama received 70 percent of the vote to Keyes' 27 percent, the largest electoral victory in Illinois history. With his win, Obama became only the third African-American elected to the U.S. Senate since Reconstruction.

Sworn into office on January 3, 2005, Obama partnered with Republican Senator Richard Lugar of Indiana on a bill that expanded efforts to destroy weapons of mass destruction in Eastern Europe and Russia. Then, with Republican Senator Tom Coburn of Oklahoma, he created a website to track all federal spending. Obama also spoke out for victims of Hurricane Katrina, pushed for alternative energy development and championed improved veterans' benefits.

His second book, The Audacity of Hope: Thoughts on Reclaiming the American Dream, was published in October 2006. The work discussed Obama's visions for the future of America, many of which became talking points for his eventual presidential campaign. Shortly after its release, the book hit No. 1 on both the New York Times and Amazon.com best-seller lists.

2008 Presidential Election

In February 2007, Obama made headlines when he announced his candidacy for the 2008 Democratic presidential nomination. He was locked in a

11

tight battle with former first lady and then-U.S. senator from New York Hillary Rodham Clinton. On June 3, 2008, Obama became the Democratic Party's presumptive nominee after winning a sufficient number of pledged delegates during the primaries, and Clinton delivered her full support to Obama for the duration of his campaign. On November 4, 2008, Barack Obama defeated Republican presidential nominee John McCain, 52.9 percent to 45.7 percent, to win election as the 44th president of the United States—and the first African-American to hold this office. His running mate, Delaware Senator Joe Biden, became vice president. Obama's inauguration took place on January 20, 2009.

When Obama took office, he inherited a global economic recession, two ongoing foreign wars and the lowest-ever international favorability rating for the United States. He campaigned on an ambitious agenda of financial reform, alternative energy and reinventing education and health care—all while bringing down the national debt. Because these issues were intertwined with the economic well-being of the nation, he believed all would have to be undertaken simultaneously. During his inauguration speech, Obama summarized the situation by saying, "Today I say to you that the challenges we face are real. They are serious and they are many. They will not be met easily or in a short span of time. But know this, America: They will be met."

First 100 Days

Between Inauguration Day and April 29, 2009, the Obama administration took action on many fronts. Obama coaxed Congress to expand health care insurance for children and provide legal protection for women seeking equal pay. A $787 billion stimulus bill was passed to promote short-term economic growth. Housing and credit markets were put on life support, with a market-based plan to buy U.S. banks' toxic assets. Loans were made to the auto industry, and new regulations were proposed for Wall Street. Obama also cut taxes for working families, small businesses and first-time home buyers. The president also loosened the ban on embryonic stem cell research and moved ahead with a $3.5 trillion budget plan.

Over his first 100 days in office, President Obama also undertook a complete overhaul of America's foreign policy. He reached out to improve relations with Europe, China, and Russia and to open dialogue with Iran, Venezuela and Cuba. He lobbied allies to support a global economic stimulus package. He committed an additional 21,000 troops to Afghanistan and set an August 2010 date for withdrawal of nearly all U.S. troops from Ira□. In more dramatic incidents, he ordered an attack on pirates off the coast of Somalia and prepared the nation for a swine flu outbreak. He signed an executive order banning excessive interrogation techniques and ordered the closing of the military detention facility at Cuba's Guantanamo Bay within a year (a deadline that ultimately would not be met). For his efforts, the Nobel Committee in Norway awarded Obama the 2009 Nobel Peace Prize.

2010 State of the Union

On January 27, 2010, President Obama delivered his first State of the Union speech. During his oration, Obama addressed the challenges of the economy, proposed a fee for larger banks, announced a possible freeze on government spending in the following fiscal year and spoke against the Supreme Court's reversal of a law capping campaign finance spending. He also challenged politicians to stop thinking of re-election and start making positive changes. He criticized Republicans for their refusal to support any legislation and chastised Democrats for not pushing hard enough to get legislation passed. He also insisted that, despite obstacles, he was determined to help American citizens through the nation's current domestic difficulties. "We don't □uit. I don't □uit," he said. "Let's seize this moment to start anew, to carry the dream forward, and to strengthen our union once more."

Challenges and Successes

In the second part of his first term as president, Obama faced a number of obstacles and scored some victories as well. In spite of opposition from Congressional Republicans and the populist Tea Party movement, Obama signed his health care reform plan, known as the Affordable Care Act, into law in March 2010. The new law prohibited the denial of coverage based on pre-existing conditions allowed citizens under 26 years old to be insured under parental plans, provided for free health screenings for certain citizens and expanded insurance coverage and access to medical care to millions of Americans. Opponents of the Affordable Care Act, which foes dubbed "Obamacare," asserted that it added new costs to the country's overblown budget, violated the Constitution with its requirement for individuals to obtain insurance and amounted to a "government takeover" of health care

On the economic front, Obama worked to steer the country through difficult financial times. After drawn-out negotiations with Republicans who gained control of the U.S. House of Representatives in the 2010 mid-term elections, he signed the Budget Control Act of 2011 in an effort to rein in government spending and prevent the government from defaulting on its financial obligations. The act also called for the creation of a bipartisan committee to seek solutions to the country's fiscal issues, but the group failed to reach any agreement on how to solve these problems.

Also in 2011, Obama signed a repeal of the military policy known as "Don't Ask, Don't Tell," which prevented openly gay troops from serving in the U.S. Armed Forces. In March 2011, he approved U.S. participation in NATO airstrikes to support rebels fighting against the forces of Libyan dictator Muammar al-Qaddafi, and in May he also gave the green light to a covert operation in Pakistan that led to the killing of infamous al-Qaeda leader Osama bin Laden by a team of U.S. Navy SEALs.

Obama gained a legal victory in June 2012 when the U.S. Supreme Court upheld the Affordable Care Act's individual mandate, which re□uired citizens to purchase health insurance or pay a tax. In a 5-4 decision, the court decided the health care law's signature provision fell within the taxation power granted to Congress under the Constitution. Voting with the majority were two associate justices appointed by Obama—Sonia Sotomayor (confirmed in 2009) and Elena Kagan (confirmed in 2010).

2012 Re-Election

As he did in 2008, during his campaign for a second presidential term, Obama focused on grassroots initiatives. Celebrities such as Anna Wintour and Sarah Jessica Parker aided the president's campaign by hosting fund-raising events.

"I guarantee you, we will move this country forward," Obama stated in June 2012, at a campaign event in Maryland. "We will finish what we started. And we'll remind the world just why it is that the United States of America is the greatest nation on Earth."

In the 2012 election, Obama faced Republican opponent Mitt Romney and Romney's vice-presidential running mate, U.S. Representative Paul Ryan. On November 6, 2012, Obama won a second four-year term as president by receiving nearly five million more votes than Romney and capturing more than 60 percent of the Electoral College.

Nearly one month after President Obama's re-election, the nation endured one of its most tragic school shootings to date when 20 children and six adults were shot to death at the Sandy Hook Elementary School in Newtown, Connecticut, on December 14, 2012. Two days after the attack, Obama delivered a speech at an interfaith vigil for the victims in Newtown and discussed a need for change in order to make schools safer while alluding to implementing stricter gun-control measures. "These tragedies must end," Obama stated. "In the coming weeks, I'll use whatever power this office holds to engage my fellow citizens—from law enforcement, to mental-health professionals, to parents and educators—in an effort aimed at preventing more tragedies like this, because what choice do we have? We can't accept events like these as routine. Are we really prepared to say that we're powerless in the face of such carnage, that the politics are too hard?"

Obama achieved a major legislative victory on January 1, 2013, when the Republican-controlled House of Representatives approved a bipartisan agreement on tax increases and spending cuts, in an effort to avoid the looming fiscal cliff crisis (the Senate voted in favor of the bill earlier that day). The agreement marked a productive first step toward the president's re-election promise of reducing the federal deficit by raising taxes on the extremely wealthy—individuals earning more than $400,000 per year and couples earning more than $450,000, according to the bill. Prior to the bill's passage, in late 2012, tense negotiations between Republicans and Democrats over spending cuts and tax increases became a bitter political battle until Vice President Joe Biden managed to hammer out a deal with Republican Senate Minority Leader Mitch McConnell. Obama pledged to sign the bill into law.

Second Term

Barack Obama officially began his second term on January 21, 2013, when U.S. Chief Justice John Roberts administered the oath of office. The inauguration was held on Martin Luther King Jr. Day, and civil-rights activist Myrlie Evers-Williams, the widow of Medgar Evers, gave the invocation. James Taylor, Beyoncé Knowles and Kelly Clarkson sang at the ceremony, and poet Richard Blanco read his poem "One Today."

In his inaugural address, Obama called the nation to action on such issues as climate change, health care, and marriage eꞏuality. "We must act, knowing that our work will be imperfect. We must act, knowing that today's victories will be only partial and that it will be up to those who stand here in four

16

years and 40 years and 400 years hence to advance the timeless spirit once conferred to us in a spare Philadelphia hall," Obama told the crowd gathered in front of the U.S. Capitol building.

The Obamas attended two official inauguration balls, including one held at the Walter E. Washington Convention Center. There the first couple danced to the Al Green classic "Let's Stay Together," sung by Jennifer Hudson. Alicia Keys and Jamie Foxx also performed.

After the inauguration, Obama led the nation through many challenges—none more difficult, perhaps, than the terrorist bombings of the Boston Marathon on April 15, 2013, which killed three people and left more than 200 injured. At a memorial service in Boston three days after the bombings, he told the wounded, "Your country is with you. We will all be with you as you learn to stand and walk and, yes, run again. Of that, I have no doubt. You will run again." And he applauded the city's response to the tragedy. "You've shown us, Boston, that in the face of evil, Americans will lift up what's good. In the face of cruelty, we will choose compassion."

In the same month, Obama also found his efforts for gun-control measures thwarted in Congress. He had supported legislation calling for universal background checks on all gun purchases and a ban on sales of assault weapons and high-capacity magazines. When the bill was blocked and withdrawn, Obama called it "a pretty shameful day for Washington."

By June, Obama had suffered a significant drop in his approval ratings in a CNN/ORC International poll. In the wake of allegations of the Internal Revenue Service targeting conservative political organizations seeking tax-exempt status and accusations of a cover-up in the terrorist killings of U.S. Ambassador to Libya Christopher Stevens and three others at a diplomatic post in Benghazi, Libya, Obama's approval rating declined to only 45 percent—his lowest rating in more than 18 months.

Experts also attributed the ratings slide to new revelations about the extent of the U.S. National Security Agency's surveillance program. Obama defended the NSA's email monitoring and telephone wiretapping during a visit to Germany that June. "We are not rifling through the emails of German citizens or American citizens or French citizens or anyone else," he said. "The encroachment on privacy has been strictly limited." Obama stated that the program had helped stop roughly 50 threats.

In early July 2013, President Obama made history when he joined former President George W. Bush in Africa to commemorate the 15th anniversary of al-Qaeda's first attack on American targets, the U.S. embassies in Tanzania and Kenya. The event marked the first meeting between two U.S. presidents on foreign soil in commemoration of an act of terrorism.

Later that month, Obama spoke out about the outrage that followed a Florida jury's decision to acquit George Zimmerman in the murder of African-American teen Trayvon Martin. "When Trayvon Martin was first shot, I said that this could have been my son," the president remarked at a White House press conference. "Another way of saying that is Trayvon Martin could have been me 35 years ago." Obama explained that this particular case was a state matter, but he discussed how the federal government could address some of the legislative and racial issues highlighted by the incident.

International Challenges

Obama found himself grappling with an international crisis in late August and September 2013 when it was discovered that Syrian leader Bashar al-Assad had used chemical weapons against civilians. While saying that thousands of people, including over 400 children, had been killed in the chemical attacks, Obama called Syria's actions "a serious national security threat to the United States and to the region, and as a conse uence, Assad and Syria needs to be held accountable."

18

The president worked to persuade Congress and the international community at large to take action against Syria but found a majority on Capitol Hill opposed to military involvement. Obama then announced an alternative solution on September 10, 2013, by stating that if al-Assad agreed with the stipulations outlined in a proposal made by Russia to give up its chemical weapons, then a direct strike against the nation could be avoided. Al-Assad acknowledged the possession of chemical weapons and ultimately accepted the Russian proposal.

Later that month, Obama made diplomatic strides with Iran. He spoke with Iranian President Hassan Rouhani on the phone, which marked the first direct contact between the leaders of the two countries in more than 30 years. This groundbreaking move by Obama was seen by many as a sign of thawing in the relationship between the United States and Iran. "The two of us discussed our ongoing efforts to reach an agreement over Iran's nuclear program," reported Obama at a press conference in which he expressed optimism that a deal could be reached to lift sanctions on Iran in return for that country's willingness to halt its nuclear development program.

Domestic Policies and Problems

Obama found himself struggling on the domestic front in October 2013. A dispute over the federal budget and Republican desires to defund or derail the Affordable Care Act caused a 16-day shut down of the federal government. After a deal had been reached to end the shutdown, Obama used his weekly address to express his frustration over the situation and his desire for political reform: "The way business is done in Washington has to change. Now that these clouds of crisis and uncertainty have lifted, we need to focus on what the majority of Americans sent us here to do—grow the economy, create good jobs, strengthen the middle class, lay the foundation for broad-based prosperity, and get our fiscal house in order for the long haul."

The Affordable Care Act continued to come under fire in October after the failed launch of HealthCare.gov, the website meant to allow people to find and purchase health insurance. Extra technical support was brought in to work on the troubled website, which was plagued with glitches for weeks. The health care law was also blamed for some Americans losing their existing insurance policies, despite repeated assurances from Obama that such cancellations would not occur. According to the Chicago Tribune, Obama insisted that the insurance companies—and not his legislation—caused the coverage change. "Remember, before the Affordable Care Act, these bad-apple insurers had free rein every single year to limit the care that you received, or used minor pre-existing conditions to jack up your premiums, or bill you into bankruptcy," he said.

Under mounting pressure, Obama found himself apologizing regarding some health care changes. In an interview with NBC News, he said of those who lost their insurance plans, "I am sorry that they are finding themselves in this situation based on assurances they got from me." Obama pledged to find a remedy to this problem, saying, "We are going to do everything we can to deal with folks who find themselves in a tough position as a conse□uence of this."

Managing Foreign Crises

The fall of 2013 brought Obama additional challenges in the area of foreign relations. In October 2013, German Chancellor Angela Merkel revealed that the NSA had been listening into her cell phone calls. "Spying among friends is never acceptable," Merkel told a summit of European leaders. In the wake of these controversies, Obama saw his approval rating drop to a new low in November 2013. Only 37 percent of Americans polled by CBS News approved of the job he was doing as president, while 57 percent disapproved of his handling of the job.

Echoes of the Cold War also returned after civil unrest and protests in the capital city of Kiev led to the downfall of Ukrainian President Viktor Yanukovych's administration in February 2014. Russian troops crossed into Ukraine to support pro-Russian forces and the annexation of the province of Crimea. In response, Obama ordered sanctions targeting individuals and businesses considered by the U.S. government to be Ukraine agitators or involved in the Crimean crisis. "In 2014 we are well beyond the days when borders can be redrawn over the heads of democratic leaders," Obama stated. The president said the sanctions were taken in close coordination with European allies and gave the U.S. "the flexibility to adjust our response going forward based on Russia's actions."

In addition to the ongoing troubles in Ukraine, tensions between Israelis and Palestinians erupted into violence in Gaza during the summer of 2014. At the same time, tens of thousands of Central American children were being apprehended at the U.S.-Mexico border after making the perilous crossing alone. Many Republicans called for the rapid deportation of these illegal immigrants, while others considered the situation a humanitarian crisis. Another of the president's woes came from the legislative branch. Speaker of the House John Boehner launched an effort to sue Obama for overstepping his executive powers with some of his actions regarding the Affordable Care Act.

In August 2014, Obama ordered the first airstrikes against the self-proclaimed Islamic State, also known as ISIS or ISIL, which had seized large swathes of Iraq and Syria and conducted high-profile beheadings of foreign hostages. The following month, the U.S. launched its first attacks on ISIS targets in Syria, although the president pledged to keep combat troops out of the conflict. Several Arab countries joined in the airstrikes against the extremist Islamic militant group. "The only language understood by killers like this is the language of force," Obama said in a speech to the United Nations. "So the United States of America will work with a broad coalition to dismantle this network of death."

21

Presidency After 2014 Elections

That November, Obama had to cope with new challenges on the home front. Republicans made an impressive showing on Election Day and gained a majority in the Senate, meaning that Obama would have to contend with Republicans controlling both houses of Congress for the final two years of his term.

Obama flexed his presidential power in December by moving to re-establish diplomatic relations with Cuba for the first time in more than 50 years. The policy change came after the exchange of American citizen Alan Gross and another unnamed American intelligence agent for three Cuban spies. In a speech at the White House, Obama explained that the dramatic shift in Cuban policy would "create more opportunities for the American and Cuban people and begin a new chapter among the nations of the Americas."

In renewing diplomatic ties with Cuba, Obama announced plans "to increase travel, commerce and the flow of information to and from Cuba." The long-standing U.S. economic embargo on Cuba, however, remained in effect and could only be removed with the approval of Congress. Obama may not be able to sway Congress to agree on this policy shift as leading Republicans—including Boehner, McConnell and Florida Senator Marco Rubio—all spoke out against Obama's new Cuba policies.

In his 2015 State of the Union address, Obama declared that the nation was out of recession. "America, for all that we've endured; for all the grit and hard work re□uired to come back . . . know this: The shadow of crisis has passed," he said. He went on to share his vision for ways to improve the nation through free community college programs and middle-class tax breaks.

With Democrats outnumbered by Republicans in both the House and the Senate, Obama threatened to use his executive power to prevent any tinkering by the opposition on his existing policies. "We can't put the security of families at risk by taking away their health insurance, or unraveling the new rules on Wall Street, or refighting past battles on immigration when we've got to fix a broken system," he said. "And if a bill comes to my desk that tries to do any of these things, I will veto it."

Not long after his State of the Union address, Obama traveled to India to meet with Prime Minister Narendra Modi. According to several news reports, Obama and Modi had reached a "breakthrough understanding" regarding India's nuclear power efforts. Obama told the Indian people in a speech given in New Delhi that "we can finally move toward fully implementing our civil nuclear agreement, which will mean more reliable electricity for Indians and cleaner, non-carbon energy that helps fight climate change." This agreement would also open the door to U.S. investment in India's energy industry.

Supreme Court Victories

The summer of 2015 brought two major U.S. Supreme Court wins for the Obama administration. The court upheld part of the president's Affordable Care Act regarding health care tax subsidies. Without these tax credits, buying medical insurance might have become too costly for millions of Americans.

On June 26, the U.S. Supreme Court also made marriage equality a reality with its 5-4 decision to overturn an earlier 6th Circuit Court of Appeals ruling that same-sex marriage bans in several states were constitutional. By reversing this earlier decision, the Supreme Court made same-sex marriage legal throughout the country. President Obama, who became the first president to voice support for same-sex marriage in May 2012, praised the court for affirming "that the Constitution guarantees marriage equality. In doing so, they've reaffirmed that all Americans are entitled to the equal protection of the law. That all people should be treated equally, regardless of who they are or who they love."

In his speech, Obama also said that the court's decision "is a conse☐uence of the countless small acts of courage of millions of people across decades who stood up, who came out, who talked to parents—parents who loved their children no matter what. Folks who were willing to endure bullying and taunts, and stayed strong . . . and slowly made an entire country realize that love is love."

On the same day as this landmark decision, President Obama grappled with an incident of racial violence by speaking at the funeral of Reverend Clementa Pinckney, one of the nine African-Americans killed by a young white man during a Bible study meeting at the Emanuel AME Church in Charleston, South Carolina. In his eulogy for Pinckney, Obama said that the church's late pastor "embodied the idea that our Christian faith demands deeds and not just words."

Iran Nuclear Deal

In July 2015, Obama announced that, after lengthy negotiations, the United States and five world powers had reached an agreement with Iran over its nuclear program. The deal would allow inspectors entry into Iran to make sure the country kept its pledge to limit its nuclear program and enrich uranium at a much lower level than would be needed for a nuclear weapon. In return, the U.S. and its partners would remove the tough sanctions imposed on Iran and allow the country to ramp up sales of oil and access frozen bank accounts.

As the administration began its effort to lobby Congress to endorse the deal, Obama made his first trip as president back to his father's homeland of Kenya. In addition to having dinner with three-dozen relatives, some of whom he met for the very first time, Obama proudly proclaimed to a packed arena, "I am proud to be the first American president to come to Kenya—and of course, I'm the first Kenyan-American to be president of the United States."

Clean Power Plan

In August 2015, the Obama administration announced The Clean Power Plan, a major climate change plan aimed at reducing greenhouse gas emissions, the first-ever national standards to limit carbon pollution from coal-burning power plants in the United States. President Obama called the plan the "single most important step that America has ever made in the fight against global climate change."

The plan calls for aggressive Environmental Protection Agency regulations including requiring existing power plants to cut carbon dioxide emissions 32 percent from 2005 levels by 2030 and use more renewable energy sources like wind and solar power. Under the regulations, states will be allowed to create their own plans to reduce emissions and are re☐uired to submit initial plans by 2016 and final versions by 2018.

Critics ☐uickly voiced loud opposition to the plan including Kentucky Senator Mitch McConnell, the Republican majority leader, who sent a letter to every governor in the United States urging them not to comply with the regulations. States and private companies, which rely on coal production for their economic livelihoods, are also expected to legally challenge the plan.

Despite the backlash from those sectors, President Obama remained steadfast in his bold action to address climate change. "We've heard these same stale arguments before," he said in an address from the White House. "Each time they were wrong."

He added: "We're the first generation to feel the impact of climate change and the last generation that can do something about it."

2015 Paris Climate Conference

In November 2015, Obama further demonstrated his commitment to environmental issues as a primary player in the international COP21 summit held outside of Paris, France. Addressing the gathered representatives of nearly 200 countries, Obama acknowledged the United States' position as the second-largest climate polluter and the nation's primary responsibility to do something about it. The resulting Paris Agreement re□uires all participating nations to reduce greenhouse gas emissions in an effort to limit the rise of global temperatures over the ensuing century and also to allocate resources for the research and development of alternative energy sources. President Obama praised the agreement for establishing the "enduring framework the world needs to solve the climate crisis" and pledged that the United States would cut its emissions more than 25 percent by 2030. In September 2016, the United States and China, the two largest emitters of greenhouse gases, announced that their countries would ratify the Paris Agreement. One month later on October 5, 2016, the United Nations announced that the agreement had been ratified by a sufficient number of countries to allow it to take effect starting on November 4, 2016.

Speaking from the Rose Garden at the White House, President Obama said: "Today, the world meets the moment, and if we follow through on the commitments that this Paris Agreement embodies, history may well judge it as a turning point for our planet."

"One the reasons I ran for this office was to make America the leader in this mission," he continued, adding he was hopeful the historic agreement could make a difference. "This gives us the best possible shot to save the one planet we've got."

On June 1, 2017, President Donald Trump, Obama's successor who was elected in November 2016, made good on his campaign promise to withdraw from the Paris Climate Agreement. With his decision, the United States joined Syria and Nicaragua as the only three countries to reject the accord. "In order to fulfill my solemn duty to protect America and it's citizens, the United States will withdraw from the Paris Climate Accord but begin negotiations to re-enter either the Paris accord or an entirely new transaction on terms that are fair to the United States," President Trump said in a speech from the White House Rose Garden.

"We're getting out. And we will start to renegotiate and we'll see if there's a better deal. If we can, great. If we can't, that's fine."

Former president Obama responded in a statement: "The nations that remain in the Paris Agreement will be the nations that reap the benefits in jobs and industries created. I believe the United States of America should be at the front of the pack. But even in the absence of American leadership; even as this Administration joins a small handful of nations that reject the future; I'm confident that our states, cities, and businesses will step up and do even more to lead the way, and help protect for future generations the one planet we've got."

Gun Control

Entering his final year as President of the United States, in early January 2016 Obama held a press conference to announce a new series of executive orders related to gun control. Citing examples such as the 2012 mass shooting at Sandy Hook elementary school, the president shed tears as he called on Congress and the gun lobby to work with him to make the country safer. His measures, which have met with vehement opposition from members of both the Republican and Democratic Parties, as well as gun advocacy groups such as the NRA, would implement more thorough background checks for gun buyers, stricter governmental oversight and enforcement of gun laws, better information sharing regarding mental health issues as related to gun ownership and investment in gun safety technology. According to a 2015 Gallup poll, most Americans favor some kind of stricter regulations of gun sales.

Final Year in Office

Shortly after the press conference, on January 12, 2016, Barack Obama delivered what would be his final State of the Union address. Diverging from the typical policy-prescribing format, Obama's message for the American people was centered around themes of optimism in the face of adversity, asking them not to let fears about security or the future get in the way of building a nation that is "clear-eyed" and "big-hearted." This did not prevent him from taking thinly disguised jabs at Republican presidential hopefuls for what he characterized as their "cynical" rhetoric, making further allusions to the "rancor and suspicion between the parties" and his failure as president to do more to bridge that gap. But Obama also took the opportunity to tout his accomplishments, citing the Affordable Care Act, diplomatic progress with Iran and Cuba, the legalization of gay marriage and profound economic recovery as among them.

Further indicating his unwillingness to accept a "lame duck" status, two months later Obama made two important moves to attempt to cement his legacy. On March 10 he met at the White House with newly elected Canadian Prime Minister Justin Trudeau in the first official visit by a Canadian leader in nearly 20 years. Central among the topics addressed during their meeting—which also included trade, terrorism and border security—was climate change, with the two leaders promising a commitment to building an international "low-carbon global economy." Trudeau's apparent concern for environmental issues and generally liberal agenda stand in contrast to his predecessor, Stephen Harper, with whom President Obama enjoyed strained relations due in part to Obama's unwillingness to allow for the construction of the Keystone XL pipeline.

A week after his meeting with Trudeau, Obama held a press conference at the White House to present 63-year-old U.S. Court of Appeals chief judge Merrick Garland as his nominee for the Supreme Court seat vacated with the unexpected death of conservative stalwart Antonin Scalia. Though Garland is considered a moderate "consensus" candidate, his nomination was immediately rebuffed by leaders of the Republican Party, who have repeatedly stated their intention to block any nominee put forward by President Obama, fearing that such a confirmation would tip the balance toward a more liberal-leaning court. In an allusion to the political standoff, President Obama closed his remarks about Garland by saying, "I am fulfilling my constitutional duty. I'm doing my job. I hope that our senators will do their jobs, and move ⬚uickly to consider my nominee." During his presidency, Obama already filled two seats in the Supreme Court, with Sonia Sotomayor and Elena Kagan, though both were confirmed when there was a Democratic-majority Senate.

Leaving the Senate to weigh their options regarding his nomination of Merrick, President Obama set out on a historic mission to Cuba on March 20. The first sitting American president to visit the island nation since 1928, Obama made the three-day visit—accompanied by First Lady Michelle Obama and their daughters Malia and Sasha. Obama's visit was part of a larger program to establish greater cooperation between the two countries, the foundations of which were laid in late 2014 when Obama and Cuban president Raul Castro announced the normalizing of diplomatic relations for the first time since 1961. At the top of the agenda during the milestone meeting between the two leaders were human rights, the U.S.'s economic embargo on Cuba and Guantanamo Bay. Following their first conversation at the Palace of the Revolution, Castro and Obama held a joint press conference broadcast on state television during which they fielded ⬚uestions from the press. While they acknowledged its complexities, both also professed a shared optimism about the road ahead.

Farewell Address

On January 10, 2017, President Obama returned to his adopted home city of Chicago to deliver his farewell address. In his speech, Obama spoke about his early days in Chicago and his continued faith in the power of Americans who participate in their democracy. "Now this is where I learned that change only happens when ordinary people get involved, and they get engaged, and they come together to demand it," he told the cheering crowd. "After eight years as your president, I still believe that. And it's not just my belief. It's the beating heart of our American idea — our bold experiment in self-government."

The president went on to address the accomplishments of his administration. "If I had told you eight years ago that America would reverse a great recession, reboot our auto industry, and unleash the longest stretch of job creation in our history — if I had told you that we would open up a new chapter with the Cuban people, shut down Iran's nuclear weapons program without firing a shot, take out the mastermind of 9-11 — if I had told you that we would win marriage equality and secure the right to health insurance for another 20 million of our fellow citizens — if I had told you all that, you might have said our sights were set a little too high," he said. "But that's what we did. That's what you did. You were the change. The answer to people's hopes and, because of you, by almost every measure, America is a better, stronger place than it was when we started."

Obama also expressed his commitment to the peaceful transfer of power to President-Elect Donald Trump, and called on politicians and American citizens to come together despite their differences. "Understand, democracy does not require uniformity," he said. "Our founders quarreled and compromised, and expected us to do the same. But they knew that democracy does require a basic sense of solidarity – the idea that for all our outward differences, we are all in this together; that we rise or fall as one."

He also appealed for tolerance and to continue the fight against discrimination: "After my election, there was talk of a post-racial America," he said. "Such a vision, however well-intended, was never realistic. All of us have more work to do. After all, if every economic issue is framed as a struggle between a hardworking white middle class and undeserving minorities, then workers of all shades will be left fighting for scraps while the wealthy withdraw further into their private enclaves.

"If we decline to invest in the children of immigrants, just because they don't look like us, we diminish the prospects of our own children – because those brown kids will represent a larger share of America's workforce," Obama

30

continued. "Going forward, we must uphold laws against discrimination . . . But laws alone won't be enough. Hearts must change."

He also quoted Atticus Finch, the main character in Harper Lee's To Kill a Mockingbird, asking Americans to heed his advice: "You never really understand a person until you consider things from his point of view, until you climb into his skin and walk around in it."

In a tearful moment, Obama addressed his wife, Michelle, and then spoke about being the proud father of his daughters, Malia and Sasha, and expressed his gratitude for Vice President Joe Biden. Obama concluded his farewell address with a call to action: "My fellow Americans, it has been the honor of my life to serve you," he said. "I won't stop; in fact, I will be right there with you, as a citizen, for all my remaining days. But for now, whether you are young or whether you're young at heart, I do have one final ask of you as your president — the same thing I asked when you took a chance on me eight years ago. I am asking you to believe. Not in my ability to bring about change — but in yours."

On January 19, 2017, Obama's last full day in office, he announced 330 commutations for nonviolent drug offenders. The presidents granted a total of 1,715 clemencies, including commuting the sentence of Chelsea Manning, the U.S. Army intelligence analyst who was sentenced to 35 years in prison for leaking classified information to WikLeaks.

In his last days in the Oval Office, Obama also presented Vice President Joe Biden with the Presidential Medal of Freedom with distinction. He shared these parting words at his last press conference with the White House press corps. " . . . I believe in this country," he said. "I believe in the American people. I believe that people are more good than bad. I believe tragic things happen. I think there's evil in the world, but I think at the end of the day, if we work hard and if we're true to those things in us that feel true and feel right, that the world gets a little better each time. That's what this presidency has tried to be about.

And I see that in the young people I've worked with. I could not be prouder of them."

"And so, this is not just a matter of no drama Obama, this is what I really believe. It is true that behind closed doors, I curse more than I do publicly...and sometimes I get mad and frustrated like everybody else does, but at my core, I think we're going to be okay. We just have to fight for it, we have to work for it and not take it for granted and I know that you will help us do that."

Life After the White House

After leaving the White House, the Obama family moved to a home in the Kalorama neighborhood of Washington, DC to allow their youngest daughter Sasha to continue school there.

On January 30, 2017, the former president released his first statement after leaving office in support of the widespread demonstrations protesting President Trump's executive order that called for "extreme vetting" to "keep radical Islamic terrorists out of the United States of America." The order bans immigrants from Iraq, Syria, Iran, Sudan, Libya, Somalia and Yemen for at least 90 days, and temporarily suspended the entry of refugees for 120 days. As a result, immigrants and refugees from predominantly Muslim countries traveling to the U.S. were detained at U.S. airports, sparking protests around the country.

Former President Obama's office released a statement in which a spokesman said that "The President fundamentally disagrees with the notion of discriminating against individuals because of their faith or religion."

The statement also underscored Obama's support of American citizens getting involved in the country's democracy: "President Obama is heartened by the level of engagement taking place in communities around the country. In his final official speech as President, he spoke about the important role of citizens and how all Americans have a responsibility to be the guardians of our democracy—not just during an election but every day.

"Citizens exercising their constitutional right to assemble, organize and have their voices heard by their elected officials is exactly what we expect to see when American values are at stake."

CHAPTER 2- BARACK AND MICHELLE OBAMA LOVE STORY

In the summer of 1989, Michelle Robinson told her mother she was going to concentrate on her law career and not worry about dating. She was 25 and had just finished her first year as an associate at Sidley & Austin, a corporate law firm in her home town of Chicago. Not long after, the firm assigned her to mentor a summer associate named Barack Obama.

Even then, there was a lot of buzz about this 27-year-old prodigy from Harvard Law School. Sidley didn't usually hire first-year law students as summer associates, so Barack's arrival was noteworthy. Martha Minow, a law professor at Harvard, told her father, Newton Minow, a high-ranking partner at Sidley, that Barack was possibly the most gifted student that she had ever taught. Michelle, who'd graduated from Harvard Law herself in 1988, felt annoyed by all the chattering. Why were people surprised that a black man might be articulate and capable?

Her own skepticism took a different form. His name struck her as odd, as did the fact that he had grown up in Hawaii. She assumed he would be "strange and overly intellectual" and that she would almost certainly dislike him.

"He sounded too good to be true," she told David Mendell, author of "Obama: From Promise to Power." "I had dated alot of brothers who had this kind of reputation coming in, so I figured he was one of these smooth brothers who could talk straight and impress people. So we had lunch, and he had this bad sport jacket and a cigarette dangling from his mouth, and I thought: 'Oh, here you go. Here's this good-looking, smooth-talking guy. I've been down this road before.' "

The fact that she was Obama's mentor made her feel self-conscious. She often recounts how she resisted when Barack asked her out, saying in an interview that she felt it would be "tacky" if they started to date because they were "the only two black people" at the firm.

That, anyhow, is how the story goes: Barack and Michelle, whose last name, of course, is now Obama, both enjoy telling it. But like many personal stories that get repeated during political campaigns, it's been polished and simplified for public consumption.

As Newton Minow and others are quick to point out, Michelle and Barack were not the only black lawyers at the firm, now called Sidley Austin. Sidley made an effort to be socially progressive. The firm had a black partner, and more African American attorneys were being hired as associates every year. Even so, Minow recalls, there probably weren't more than a half-dozen, and it must have felt to Michelle as though she and Barack were under a microscope. Which, in a way, they were. Before Barack and Michelle became an official item, Minow and his wife, Jo, ran into them at the popcorn stand at a movie theater. Minow is not sure, but thinks it may have been their fabled first date to see the Spike Lee movie "Do the Right Thing." "I think they were a little embarrassed," Minow says with a laugh.

And the truth is, if Michelle resisted, it wasn't for long. Andrew Goldstein, a Sidley attorney who worked with Michelle, says he had the impression that Michelle was pursuing Barack as much as he was pursuing her, and with plenty of resources. She was tall, poised, very put-together, with an air of strength and a dazzling smile. "She is just as charismatic as he is," he says.

Another colleague, Mary Carragher, who at the time was a more senior associate assigned to work with Michelle, remembers how smitten Barack and Michelle seemed with each other. Sometimes, in the slow hours around 5:30 p.m., Carragher would go to Michelle's office to talk about a case or drop off some work, and, through the half-open door, she would see Barack, sitting on one corner of the desk. Michelle would be seated, the two of them rapt, oblivious, chatting.

"I could tell by the body language, he's just courting her," says Carragher, who would ⬚uietly depart without bothering them, thinking, 'You know what, I'm going back to my office.' "

But between Barack's visits, Michelle would confide in Carragher, sharing the tidbits she was gleaning about him. It was clear that she was now intrigued -- rather than put off -- by his unlikely origins and upbringing, which she would relay piece by piece as she learned about them. " 'I can't believe he's got a white grandmother from Kansas!' " Carragher recalls Michelle telling her.

"She had all these little facts about him," says Carragher. "She was just learning about him and getting to know him, and she seemed to be ⬚uite taken with him." His biracial heritage -- he was the son of a foreign student from Kenya and a white woman from Kansas -- was part of the appeal. "She was just sort of amazed by him."

After their first date, "We clicked right away...by the end of the date it was over...I was sold," Michelle has said.

After dating for three years, Michelle and Barack tied the knot on October 3, 1992. Of their vows, Michelle has said, "Barack didn't pledge riches, only a life that would be interesting. On that promise he delivered."

A lifelong fashion lover, Michelle Obama was stunning in an off-the-shoulder duchess satin gown with a sweetheart neckline. She accessorized dress, which also featured floral appliques, with a princess-length veil and opera gloves.

Family first- managing family life

If a week is a long time in politics, eight years seems like a lifetime - or a childhood, at least.

The couple had two children, malia and sasha. When Malia and Sasha Obama entered the White House in 2009, they were just 10 and seven years old respectively. Now, Malia is taking a gap year before entering Harvard, while Sasha is staying in Washington to complete high school.

It is a far cry from the time when they were first shown around the White House by the Bush twins in November 2008 and they concluded the visit by jumping up and down on the beds. As Michelle Obama noted last year, they have transformed from "bubbly little girls into poised young women".

While critics on both sides of the political divide might take issue with Barack Obama's time in office, most people agree the president and first lady have done a good job in ensuring their daughters have had as normal a life as possible while in the spotlight.

"You really have to credit the Obamas as great parents, whatever your politics or your views of government," Doug Wead, a former special assistant to President George H.W. Bush, said in March last year.

"I think they'll be beloved by the nation, honoured by the nation. There's just genuine bipartisan admiration for them."

Normal domestic life

From going to school to doing every day chores, keeping life "normal" was the aim from the start.

"That was the first thing I said to the White House staff: 'You know, we're going to have to set up some boundaries', because they're going to need to be able to make their beds and clean up," Mrs Obama said shortly after her husband was elected president eight years ago.

In an essay on fatherhood in 2015, Mr Obama said "the surprising truth" was that the White House had actually made family life "more normal".

When the family moved into the iconic building for the first time, Mr Obama recalled, it "was really the first time since the girls were born that we've been able to gather as a family almost every night."

One of the most important aspects of that normal life is the 6.30 pm dinners in the Family Dining Room, which Mr Obama called "sacrosanct".

"That's inviolable. My staff knows that it pretty much takes a national emergency to keep me away from that dinner table," Mr Obama said.

As mom-in-chief, Mrs Obama also regulated television time, with the girls not allowed to watch TV or use the computer during the week, unless it's for schoolwork.

They were allowed to watch more at the weekend, including reality shows like Keeping Up with the Kardashians, even if the president didn't always approve.

"When they watch that stuff, (Barack) doesn't like that as much," Mrs Obama told Hello! magazine in 2011.

School years

Having their school nearby helped. "I will never forget that winter morning as I watched our girls, just seven and ten years old, pile into those black SUVs with all those big men with guns. And I saw their little faces pressed up against the window, and the only thing I could think was, "What have we done?" Mrs Obama recalled at the Democratic National Convention last year.

The choice was influenced by conversations Mrs Obama had with Hillary Clinton and Rosalynn Carter about how best to bring up children in the public eye.

As well helping ensure they stayed out of the spotlight, it also meant Mr Obama was able to attend Malia's tennis matches and Sasha's dance recitals, as well as getting to experience "what all dads dread: watching my daughter go to her first prom. In high heels".

Mother-in-law Marian

Helping to ensure stability in their domestic life was the president's mother-in-law Marian Robinson, also known as Grandmother-in-Chief, or First Grandmother of the United States.

"Michelle calls Marian Robinson her 'rock'. She is steady, she is strong," Peter Slevin, author of Michelle Obama: A Life, told The Telegraph in 2015. "She has opinions, but she is very grounded in the real world."

Living on the third floor of the Residency of the White House - one above the president and his immediate family - Mrs Robinson has always been on hand to keep the children in check - or indulge them.

"I have candy, they stay up late," she said. "They watch television for as long as they want to. We'll play games until the wee hours. I do everything that grandmothers do that they're not supposed to," she told the Boston Globe before the family moved into the White House.

The president saw his mother-in-law's presence as essential to keeping a semblance of normality in the goldfish bowl of the White House.

"I think Mrs Robinson acts as a calming presence," Mr Slevin said. "Barack Obama talks about how much he enjoys having her in the White House. He also says because she can slip out, she comes back to the White House with stories of real life. She is a humanising presence."

As the girls grew up, her role evolved into chaperoning the girls on global trips, such as their trip to London two years ago.

'When they go low, we go high'

One of the main challenges faced by the Obamas was protecting their daughters from the vitriol hurled at their father throughout the eight years in office.

It formed the basis of Mrs Obama's widely praised speech at the Democratic National Convention last year, when her motto became a key slogan in Mrs Clinton presidential campaign.

"That is what Barack and I think about every day as we try to guide and protect our girls through the challenges of this unusual life in the spotlight," the first lady said.

"How we urge them to ignore those who question their father's citizenship or faith. How we insist that the hateful language they hear from public figures on TV does not represent the true spirit of this country. How we explain that when someone is cruel, or acts like a bully, you don't stoop to their level - no, our motto is, when they go low, we go high.

"With every word we utter, with every action we take, we know our kids are watching us. We as parents are their most important role models."

CHAPTER 3- BARACK OBAMA AND KENYA- IS HE A CLOSE MUSLIM?

Although he never lived in Africa, Barack Obama - is half Kenyan by descent. He has a Kenyan father and an American mother. Rumors say Obama still is a Muslim. What are the facts?

Barack Obama's Parents

Obama's father, Barack Hussein Obama Sr., was born in a poor town in Kenya's western Nyanza province as the son of a cook in British service. It was the kind of small village where chicken roams freely and children in rags wander around the streets. The family was from the Luo tribe. The president's father "grew up herding goats and went to school in a tin-roof shack", as himself wrote in his book "Dreams of my Father" (1995, reissued 2004).

But the father was a smart and hard-working young man, and when John F. Kennedy launched a program to offer American scholarships to promising Kenyan students, the father grabbed the opportunity with both hands. He was able to enter the University of Hawaii that way. There he met and married President Obama's mother, Ann Dunham who was a fellow student at the same university. She was a full-blooded American from Kansas, coming from a blue-collar family.

Senator Obama was born there in 1961. However, the marriage only lasted until 1965. The father went on to study at Harvard, and after that returned to Kenya to work for oil companies. He went on to become an economist in the government of Jomo Kenyatta, the first Kenyan president after independence in 1963. He died in a car accident in 1982.

The mother remarried an Indonesian oil manager, Lolo Soetoro, and together with Barack Obama (who was then 5 years old) the couple moved to Jakarta in Indonesia. When Obama was ten, he returned to his grandparents in Hawaii because of the better opportunities for education there. His father came to visit him there. It would be the last time he saw him. Eventually, after Occidental

41

College and Columbia University, Obama would enter Harvard University just like his father did.

Two Visits To Kenya

Before enrolling in Harvard, Obama visited his relatives in Kenya for the first time. His second visit in 2006, the latest to date, was an official one. Joined by his wife Michelle and his two daughters, he was received by US Ambassador Michael Rannesberger at the airport of Kenya's capital Nairobi. From there, a tour went through the city with thousands of Kenyans - proud that somebody 'from them' made it to the US Senate - cheering along the streets. A real Obama mania swept the country.

Obama also visited his 85-year old grandmother in her little village of Nyangoma-Kogelo. She cooked a traditional ugali meal for him. She didn't buy a new dress for the occasion, saying that Obama would hug her anyway, as he had done before. She doesn't speak English, so they talked through an interpreter.

Obama A Muslim?

Especially on the internet, the rumor still goes that Obama is a Muslim. That seems to be without basis in fact. Obama's grandfather converted from Christianity to Islam as a young man and added the Arab-style 'Hussein' to his name. The Senator inherited that middle name from his grandfather and father: the Senator's full name is Barack Hussein Obama like his father. Also 'Barack' has an Islamic background, meaning "blessed" in African-Arabic (East-African languages have alot of Arab words .

But Obama's father had already abandoned Islam before he met Ann Dunham in Hawaii, becoming a skeptic, atheist person at a young age like Obama's mother. Obama's stepfather, Lolo Soetoro, was nominally a Muslim but considered religion as of little importance. The Senator himself was also leaning towards skepticism until he heard a sermon delivered in . He became a Christian and in 1988 joined Trinity United Church of Christ in Chicago.

But political opponents keep circulating rumors about Obama being a closet Muslim. Even the Hillary Clinton camp fed into this by circulating a photo from Obama's Kenyan visit in 2006, with Obama wearing a traditional Somali (Muslim) costume. However, this seems to have been nothing more than Obama showing respect to his hosts and trying on the clothes that he received from them as a gift.

"In no other country on earth, is my story even possible"

During his keynote speech at the Democratic Convention in 2004, Obama drew comparisons between his background and his vision of an America with e ual opportunities for all. "In no other country on earth, is my story even possible", he said, pointing to the fact he made it to the US Senate as the son of a poor black immigrant.

There's an irony in that. In Kenya, the Kikuy tribe dominates both politics and the economy. They keep out the other tribes through favoritism and even corruption. For a (half)-Luo like Obama, it would be extremely hard to become the President of Kenya. Indeed, the election violence in Kenya of December-January 2008 precisely has this background. There's evidence that sitting President Kibaki, a Kikuyu (as well as virtually his entire administration), stole the elections of his Luo opponent Raila Odinga. This sparked the riots, as the Luo as well as other smaller tribes saw this as again a signal that the Kikuyu will conspire to keep any Luo out of office.

So Kenyans are now telling each other the joke that a Luo will sooner become the President of the United States than the President of Kenya.

CHAPTER 4- BARACK OBAMA ACCOMPLISHMENTS AS THE PRESIDENT

As the first African-American elected President of the United States, Barack Obama became a pivotal figure in American history even before his inauguration. But after winning a second term in 2012, his achievements in office have made him one of the most transformative presidents of the past hundred years. He took office with a country in peril and led it through the Great Recession, two wars, civil unrest, a rash of mass shootings, and changing cultural demographics. In the 2008 campaign, he called for change and eight years later we are living in a more prosperous country because of it.

Here are 28 of President Obama's biggest accomplishments as President of the United States.

1 – Rescued the country from the Great Recession, cutting the unemployment rate from 10% to 4.7% over six years

2 – Signed the Affordable Care Act which provided health insurance to over 20 million uninsured Americans

3 – Ended the war in Iraq

4 – Ordered for the capture and killing of Osama Bin Laden

5 – Passed the $787 billion America Recovery and Reinvestment Act to spur economic growth during the Great Recession

6 – Supported the LGBT community's fight for marriage e uality

7 – Commuted the sentences of nearly 1200 drug offenders to reverse "unjust and outdated prison sentences"

8 – Saved the U.S. auto industry

9 – Helped put the U.S. on track for energy independence by 2020

10 – Began the drawdown of troops in Afghanistan

11 – Signed the Deferred Action for Childhood Arrivals allowing as many as 5 million people living in the U.S. illegally to avoid deportation and receive work permits

12 –Signed the Dodd-Frank Wall Street Reform and Consumer Protection Act to re-regulate the financial sector

13 – Dropped the veteran homeless rate by 50 percent

14 – Reversed Bush-era torture policies

15 – Began the process of normalizing relations with Cuba

16 – Increased Department of Veteran Affairs funding

17 – Signed the Credit Card Accountability, Responsibility, and Disclosure Act

18 – Boosted fuel efficiency standards for cars

19 – Improved school nutrition with the Healthy Hunger-Free Kids Act

20 – Repealed the military's "Don't Ask, Don't Tell" policy

21 – Signed the Hate Crimes Prevention Act, making it a federal crime to assault anyone based on sexual or gender identification

22 – Helped negotiate the landmark Iran Nuclear Deal

23 – He signed the Lilly Ledbetter Fair Pay Act to combat pay discrimination against women

24 – Nominated Sonia Sotomayor to the Supreme Court, making her the first Hispanic ever to serve as a justice

25 – Supported veterans through a $78 billion tuition assistance GI bill

26 – Won the Nobel Peace Prize in 2009 "for his extraordinary efforts to strengthen international diplomacy and cooperation between peoples"

27 – Launched My Brother's Keeper, a White House initiative designed to help young minorities achieve their full potential

28 – Expanded embryonic stem cell research leading to groundbreaking work in areas including spinal injury treatment and cancer

CHAPTER 5- SURPRISING FACTS ABOUT BARACK OBAMA

1. His full name is Barack Hussein Obama II. He is the 44th US President. However, he is the first African American to hold that position. He is also the first US President who is not born in Continental USA.

2. Barack Obama was named as Nobel Peace Prize Laureate of 2009 only 9 months after he became the President of America.

3. He visited a Federal prison and he was USA's first sitting President to have done so.

4. In a period of almost last 100 years, he is USA's first sitting President to have visited Cuba.

5. Guantanamo Bay detention camp was ordered to be closed by President Obama only few days after he took charge of the office. Interestingly, the congress prevented the closing of the camp.

6. The Twitter followers of Obama in 2016 was the highest among any world leader.

7. China has something called OFC. What does that stand for? It stands for Obama Fried Chicken!

8. Obama is a left-handed person. Well, he is not alone. There are several other famous people who are left-handed. Some names will be Da Vinci, Napoleon, Bill Gates, Michelangelo, Einstein, Oprah, Newton and Jimi Hendrix.

9. There is an Islamist militant group is Somalia. The group did something funny in 2012. It declared a bounty of 10 camels for Barack Obama and a bounty of 2 camels for anyone who brings information on Hillary Clinton.

10. Robert F. Kennedy, in 1961 predicted that in coming 40 years, US will have a black president and he was correct except that his prediction was not entirely correct. It took 46 years before Obama became President.

11. 71 years after Hiroshima bombing, Barack Obama was USA's first sitting President to visit the place.

12. In his inaugural address, President Obama uttered the words Gay Rights (emphasis on Gay). He was the first US President to do so.

13. He published an academic paper after becoming US President. He was the USA's first sitting President to have done so.

14. He addresses David Cameron – Prime Minister of the UK as 'Bro'.

15. As mentioned earlier, President Barack Obama was born outside Continental USA. He was actually born in Honolulu, Hawaii. His date of birth is August 4, 1961 (that's the same year when Robert F. Kennedy predicted that USA will have a Black President in 40 years).

16. President Obama's father was from Kenya. His father's name was Barack Obama Sr. who was an economist in Kenyan government.

17. President Obama's mother's name was Stanley Ann Dunham who was from Kansas, USA.

18. When Barack Obama was just 2 years old, his mother and father got divorced. His mother married another man named Lolo Soetoro. However, Obama didn't stay with his mother and stepfather. He spent most of his childhood in Hawaii with his maternal grandparents.

19. He studied in Occidental College in Los Angeles. Then he went to Columbia University in New York and finally studied at Harvard Law School.

20. He worked as a teacher as well as civil-rights lawyer before becoming President of USA. He even worked as telemarketer, was into construction field, worked at law firms and even sold island trinkets when he was in Hawaii.

A Surprising Barack Obama Fact: He used cocaine and marijuana as a teenager. Before running for presidency, he promised his wife that he had ☐uit smoking, which was a lie. However, eventually he quit smoking in 2010 because he wanted to be a good father.

CONCLUSION

While every U.S. President has a somewhat different story than the average American, President Obama's story stands out, even among this group. Born in Hawaii, he was born of two University of Hawaii students. His mother was American, and his father, a Kenyan student from Nyanza Province who was studying in America. The early 1960's was a difficult time for interracial marriages, and the young Obama's faced tremendous pressure. This, among other things culminated in the couple's divorce when young Barack was only 2 years old.

His mother then met and fell in love with an Indonesian man studying for his master's degree, Lolo Soetoro. Soon they were married and the family then relocated to Jakarta, Indonesia. At the time of the move, Barack was 6. While there, they had a daughter, Barack's half sister, Maya. While in Indonesia, Barack attended a private Catholic School, SD Assisi. He later attended another excellent elementary school, SD Besuki Menteng. After 4 years in Indonesia, Barack moved back to Hawaii and lived with his maternal grandmother.

After moving back to Hawaii, he fre□uently played basketball, a sport at which he excelled, and enjoys playing to this day. By most accounts, he is still □uite good. He even played on his school' s well-regarded varsity team, although he wasn't a starter. While in high school he worked at a Baskin-Robins ice cream shop.

After graduating from high school, he moved to Los Angeles, California, where he attended Occidental College for 2 years. He got good grades, and after his sophomore year, transferred to Columbia University in New York. At this prestigious, Ivy League school, he again excelled, and graduated with his political science degree.

Barack Obama's Early Political Career

Barack has reached the pinnacle of U.S. politics, being elected President of the United States in 2008. However, he started out far more modestly, back in his adopted home city of Chicago. He won his Illinois Senate seat in 1996, after he manages to get all his opponents dis□ualified. As he was the only candidate on the ballot, he won easily.

In 1999, Obama began his fight for the U.S. Congressional seat of Rep. Bobby Rush. He lost that contest in 2000, but was determined to continue his □uest for a Federal government office. To that end, Mr. Obama set his sights on the U.S. Senate.in 2003, in preparation for the 2004 election.

He again managed to receive significant assistance from the press and the missteps of his opponents. His main challenger for the Democratic primary was ousted due to a sex scandal that the Obama campaign was only too happy to assist the media in reporting. Again, the future president used what some consider "dirty" tactics to help secure a nomination.

That was only the beginning, however. Later in the campaign, after he had won the Democratic primary, he again received substantial assistance due to an opponent's scandal, which his campaign was the beneficiary of. This time it was his Republican opponent in the 2004 Senate campaign who fell by the wayside, actually withdrawing from the election, and paving the way for an unopposed Obama victory. He was now a U.S. Senator.

If anyone thought he would receive such an easy victory in his run for the Presidency, they would be mistaken. Although he had very limited governmental experience, and no leadership experience in the private sector, Mr. Obama is undeterred in seeking the Democratic Party's presidential nomination for 2008.

Simple facts about Barack Obama -

Barack Obama

44th President of the United States (D)

Date of Birth:

August 4, 1961

Place of Birth:

Honolulu, Hawaii

Parents:

Mother - Ann Dunham, Father - Barack Obama Sr. (Divorced when Barack was 2 yrs old)

Barack lived with grandparents (Madelyn and Stanley Dunham) in Hawaii from the age of 10

Wife:

Michelle, born 1963 - Married Barack on 10/18/1992

Children:

Mailia Ann, born 1998

Natasha, born 2001

High School Education:

Punahou Academy - Honolulu, HI - Graduating Class of 1979

College Education:

BA-political science, Columbia University, 1983

Law School:

Harvard, 1991, editor and president of the Harvard Law Review

Employment:

Director, Developing Communities Project (DCP), 1985 - 1988

Lecturer, Constitutional Law, University of Chicago 1992 - 2004

Government:

Illinois State Senate, 1997 - 2004

United States Senate, 2004 - 2008

President of the United States, 2009-

Barack Obama Books:

The president is a best selling author. He has authored 2 books.

The first was Dreams from My Father: A Story of Race and Inheritance

Published by Times Books in 1995, and the second, The Audacity of

Hope: Thoughts on Reclaiming the American Dream (Vintage),published in 2006

by Crown Publishing. They have been very successful and probably won't be his

last.

Barack Obama Quotes - A Window Into His Soul?

Much can be discovered about a person by the original things which they

say. Here are some of Barack Obama's quotes. They give us a good glimpse into

the man himself.

"A good compromise, a good piece of legislation, is like a good sentence;

or a good piece of music. Everybody can recognize it. They say, 'Huh. It works.

It makes sense.'"

"Change will not come if we wait for some other person or some other

time. We are the ones we've been waiting for. We are the change that we seek."

"Focusing your life solely on making a buck shows a certain poverty of

ambition. It asks too little of yourself. Because it's only when you hitch your

wagon to something larger than yourself that you realize your true potential."

"I cannot swallow whole the view of Lincoln as the Great Emancipator."

"I know my country has not perfected itself. At times, we've struggled to

keep the promise of liberty and equality for all of our people. We've made our

share of mistakes, and there are times when our actions around the world have

not lived up to our best intentions."

"I don't take a dime of their lobbyist money, and when I am president,

they won't find a job in my White House."

"If the people cannot trust their government to do the job for which it exists - to protect them and to promote their common welfare - all else is lost."

Barack Obama's list of accomplishments will not stop with his presidency. After that chapter in his life concludes, it will only be the doorway to the next step in his path to more amazing things.

Life after the presidency

What's it like to deal with normal life after eight years under the harshest scrutiny possible? Barack and Michelle Obama are figuring that out, and it apparently involves lots of golf and SoulCycle.

These days, they still have a staff of 20 people and have an office in the West End of Washington, D.C. Both the Obamas are writing books, and they're also planning the Obama Presidential Center in Chicago's South Side. Politically, President Obama is expected to help support Democrats during the midterm elections in 2018.

President Obama still can't drive because of security concerns, and that was something he was looking forward to doing outside of office. But he's still happy with a smaller security force. "If he wants to go out to dinner on a Saturday, that doesn't take teams of people and hours of advance," his chief of staff, Anita Breckenridge, told People. "You know? That's really freeing."

As for the cool leather jacket President Obama wore in March, to the delight of the Internet? He apparently had it all this time, but felt it wasn't presidential to wear it while he was in office:

Michelle is enjoying going to SoulCycle, and naturally, brings a healthy packed lunch with her every day to the office. Her husband still doesn't ☐uite know how to use the coffeemaker. But one thing remains the same: he's still close to Vice President Biden, and the two play golf every now and then. Thank goodness.

Printed in Great Britain
by Amazon

52573873R00033